A BardCode Project

Sweet Forme

Shake-Speare's Perfect Sonnets

Also by Gregory Betts

Poetry

If Language (BookThug, 2005)
Haikube (BookThug, 2006)
The Others Raisd in Me (Pedlar Press, 2009)
Psychic Geographies and Other Topics (Quattro Press, 2010)
The Obvious Flap (with Gary Barwin, Bookthug, 2011)
This is Importance (Wolsak & Wynn, 2011)
Boycott (Make Now Press, 2014)

Nonpoetry

Avant-Garde Canadian Literature: The Early Manifestations (University of Toronto Press, 2013)
Finding Nothing: The VanGardes 1959-1975 (University of Toronto Press, forthcoming)

Editions

W.W.E. Ross: Irrealities, Sonnets & Laconics (with Barry Callaghan, Exile Editions 2003, 2012)
After Exile: A Raymond Knister Poetry Reader (Exile Editions 2003)
Lawren Harris In the Ward: His Poetry and Paintings (Exile Editions 2007, 2012)
The Wrong World: Bertram Brooker's Stories and Essays (University of Ottawa Press, 2009)
RUSH: What Fuckan Theory; A Study uv Langwage by bill bissett (with Derek Beaulieu, BookThug, 2012)
Counterblasting Canada: Marshall McLuhan, Wyndham Lewis, Sheila Watson and Wilfred Watson (with Paul Hjartarson and Kristine Smika, 2016)
Space Between Her Lips: The Selected Poetry of Margaret Christakos (Wilfrid Laurier University Press, 2017)
Avant Canada: Artists, Prophets, Revolutionaries (with Christian Bök, Wilfrid Laurier University Press, 2019)
They Have Bodies: A Realistic Novel in Five Acts by Barney Allen (University of Ottawa Press, 2020)

Sweet Forme

Shake-Speare's Perfect Sonnets

A BardCode Project

Gregory
Betts

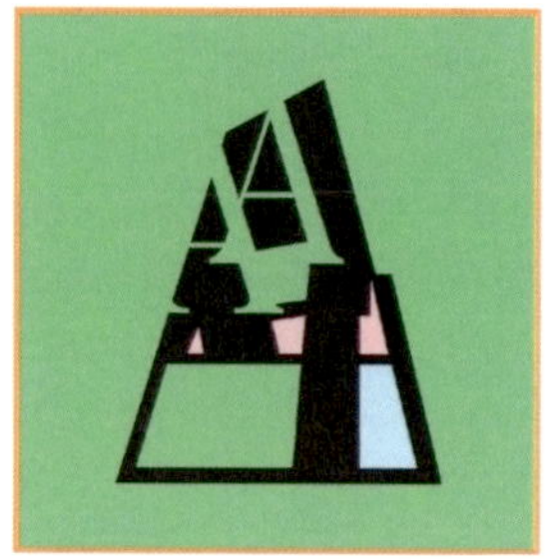

National Library of Australia
Catalogue-in-Publication entry
Gregory Betts
Sweet Forme: Shake-Speare's Perfect Sonnets
ISBN: 978-0-6488079-5-7

Published by Apothecary Archive: August, 2020
Created on Gadigal land.
Book Design: Gareth Sion Jenkins
Typeset in Roboto: 9pt, 10pt, 12pt, 14pt

E.2.

Colouring the Text

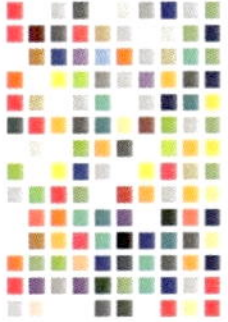

Sing this staged world within its grid. In the digital age, data grids not only structure our reception of the world, but pre-determine the boundaries of our actions and interactions, from cell-phones to traffic lights to the manufacture of products that present themselves as natural (including agriculture, of course). The grid has penetrated the world and become its unconscious legislator. You see it more brutally in so-called new world design, with gridded streets and block matrix towers, but all work in the digital age is just an elaborate series of spreadsheets and colour grids seen or unseen layered upon one another. Zoom in far enough on your screen and your text becomes blunt blocks of hues and shades.

What does the dominance of maths, however unseen, mean for art, culture, self, perspective, and time? Long before it became dominant, there was Shakespeare using the grid as medium to delve into these same questions. In 1609, he published a series of 154 sonnets called *Shake-Speare's Sonnets*. Now, from our vantage in the grid, we can recognize the sonnet as a poetics of math, the embodiment of the desire to define arbitrary frames and work within such limitations to reveal the buried structure of the world. Math sets its basic frame by the limits of just 10 digits, 0 to 9. Accordingly, the sonnet is patterned by the rhythmic frame of 5 iambic feet, hence 10 syllables skipping across a line in binary measure, da-dum da-dum da-dum da-dum da-dum. The sonnet is in fact a tightly designed grid of 10 syllables across by 14 lines down. Each syllable occupies its own cell in that structure. The poem is built by a further mathematical formula: 8 lines outlining a question, 6 lines the answer.

Wordsworth believed *Shake-Speare's Sonnets* to be autobiographical; they were his little songs, after all. I agree only to the extent that by the evidence of the poems themselves we can see that Shakespeare recognized the sonnet as a metonymy for the structural forces that shape our lives: the bios of graphs that determine the self. Pulling someone from the world into a grid affords them the timeless perfection that only abstract mathematics ought to claim (hence the regular reminders in the sonnets of the marvel of immortality offered in his poetry). He wrote the play *King Lear* at the same time as the sonnets, a play that shows the irrelevance of honour for systems. Power is binary: you either have it or you don't. The grid of being flows from that proposition. Even the plot is operational, commencing with the long division of territory into nested subsets.

We know Shakespeare was deeply invested in the meaning of the sound codes in language because of his pioneering work with the English sonnet (which we now call the Shakespearean sonnet). In the sonnet grid, the tenth column is widely understood to govern the sound structure of the work. The rhyming patterns operate as a code for cultural inheritance.

However, nobody has ever mapped the sound code (what I call the BardCode) of the other nine columns. Using the rhyme pattern of the tenth column as a sound palette I have now mapped the sound code of the entire sonnet sequence. Each of the 21, 540 syllables of his sonnets has been coded and tagged. There are, it turns out, 231 different rhyme groupings in his book.

In theatre, when rehearsing Shakespeare, actors "colour the text" when they perform exercises that release the emotional euphony of the language by dropping the consonants and over-enunciating—drawing out—the vowels. The shift and play of sounds in his writing, particularly the vowels' contrast with powerful, often repeated consonants, taxes the tongue and the jaws. His language makes athletes of actors. Instead of burying the effects, thespians learn to accentuate them so that their inherent music informs each utterance. *Sweet Forme* also colours the text to draw out the patterns and play. Each syllable has been distilled down to the root rhyme beneath the text.

The complete set was then alphabetized and assigned an rgb hex value based on a colour wheel, thus creating a heat map of tones and rhymes (shades of green sound more alike than red). The speckled (pock-marked) look of the sonnets shows the shifting tones and varied notes of its internal rhymes.

Assigning a colour to this sound code makes visible, vibrant, and readable the poems' buried sonic information. From within Shakespeare's 154 sonnets seven syllabically perfect specimens stand out—as do their insights on form, perfection, abstraction, poetry, and generation. These are poems that hold poetry up as vaccine to omnipresent ailment and decay.

In *King Lear*, the Earl of Kent lashes out at Oswald, threatening, "A plague upon your epileptic visage" (II.ii). Plague imagery and insult runs rampant throughout Shakespeare's works. Indeed, *Lear*, like the *Sonnets*, was written and published during a time of pandemic and quarantine as London reeled from the wrath of a Bubonic Plague that killed a third of the city (Shakespeare spent a total of 6.5 years in quarantine in the decade). With death surrounding him and his readers, the sonnets offer meditations on the role of art in creating an alternative to mortality; an idea of timeless, unblemished perfection.

If poetic forme aspires to perfection, the poet, in contrast, like his earthly love outside the text, must inevitably succumb to decay as the cost of his pursuit of this abstract ideal:

> My love is as a fever, longing still
> For that which longer nurseth the disease,
> Feeding on that which doth preserve the ill,
> The uncertain sickly appetite to please. ("147")

From his sacrifice to this cause, I invite you now, dear reader, to consider these timeless monuments to abstraction, the only perfect sonnets in his oeuvre, as anticipations and revelations of the meaning of the grid.

—Gregory Betts, 2020.

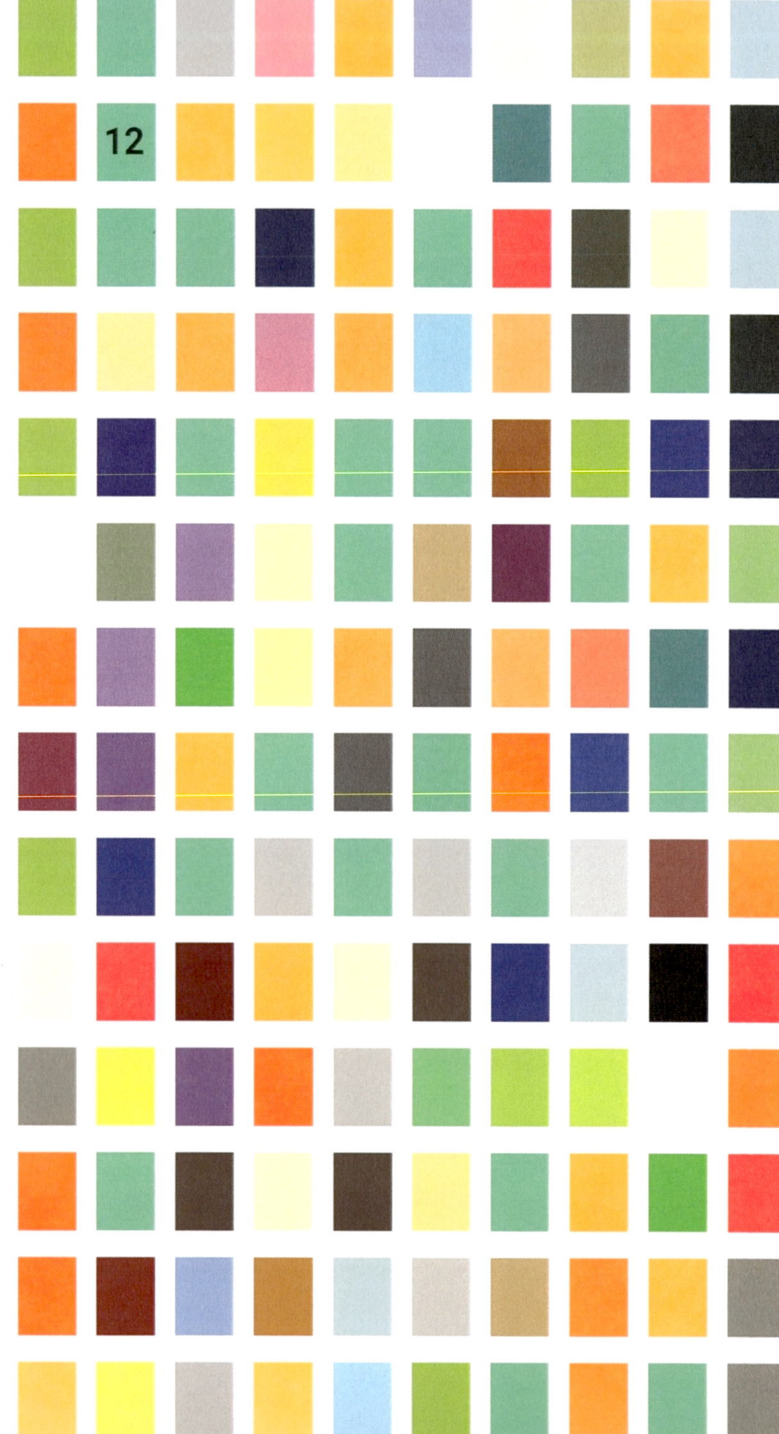

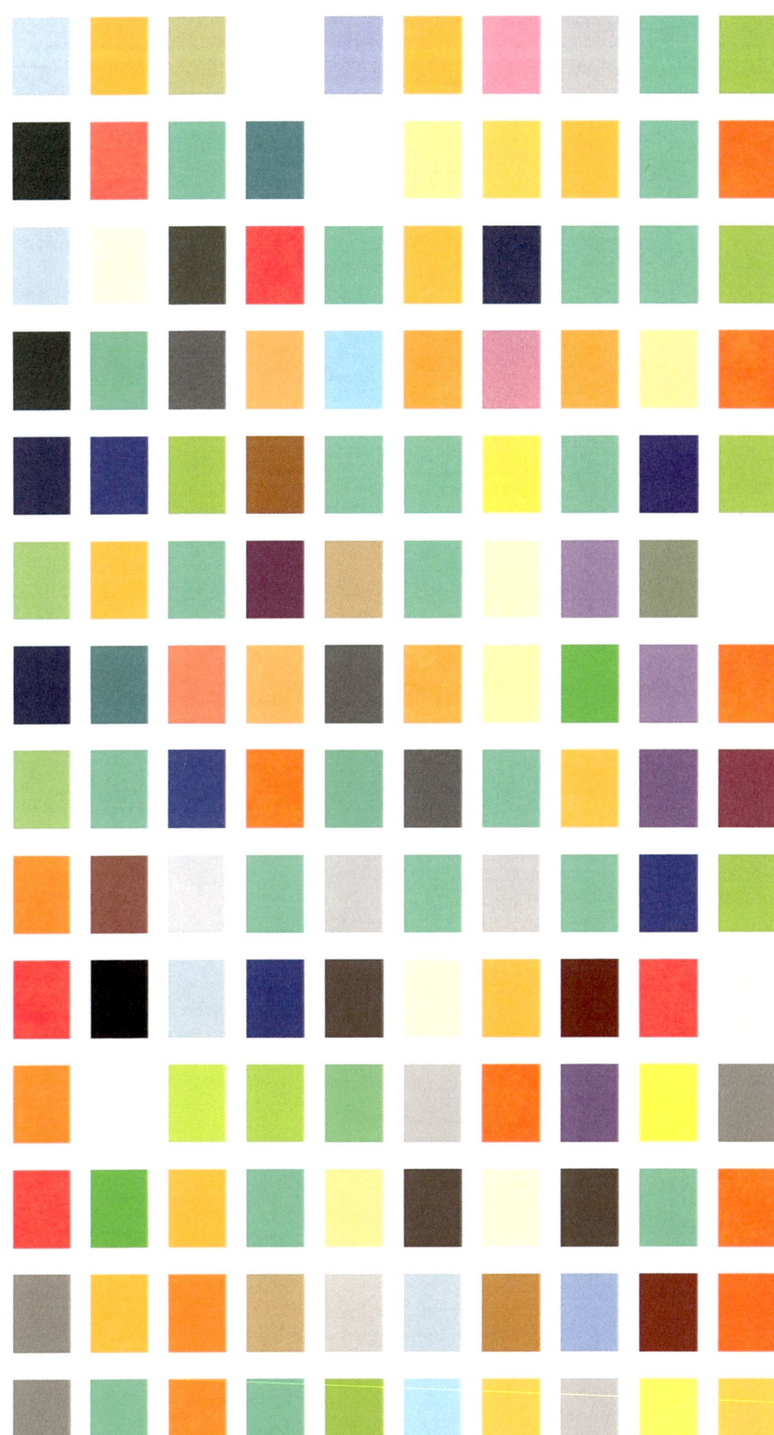

when i doe count the clock that tels the time

and see the brave day sunck in hid ious night

when i be hold the vi o let past prime

and sa ble curls all sil verd ore with white

when loft y trees i see bar ren of leaves

which erst from heat did can o pie the herd

and som mers greene all gir ded up in sheaves

borne on the beare with white and brist ly beard

then of thy beau ty do i quest ion make

that thou a mong the wastes of time must goe

since sweets and beau ties do them selves for sake

and die as fast as they see o thers grow

and no thing gainst times sieth can make de fence

save breed to brave him when he takes thee hence

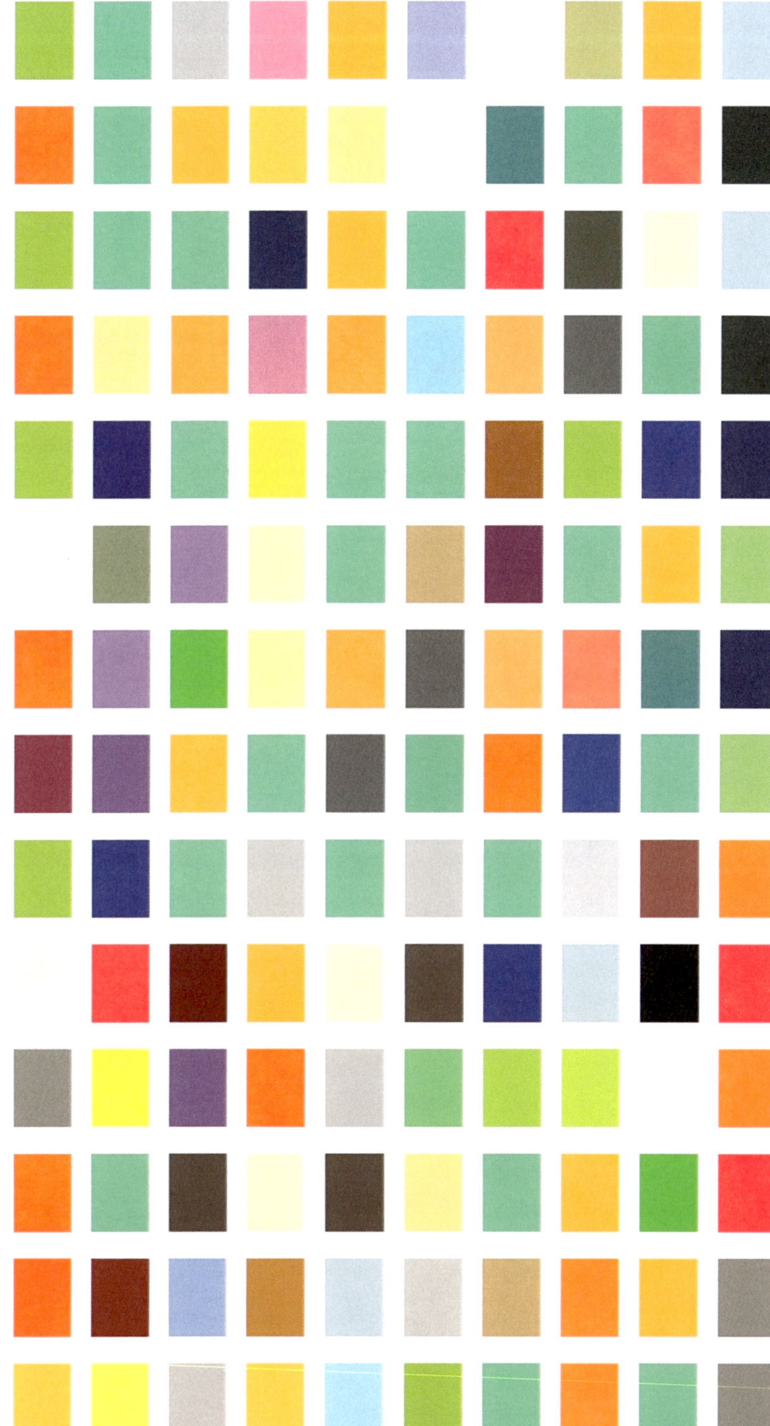

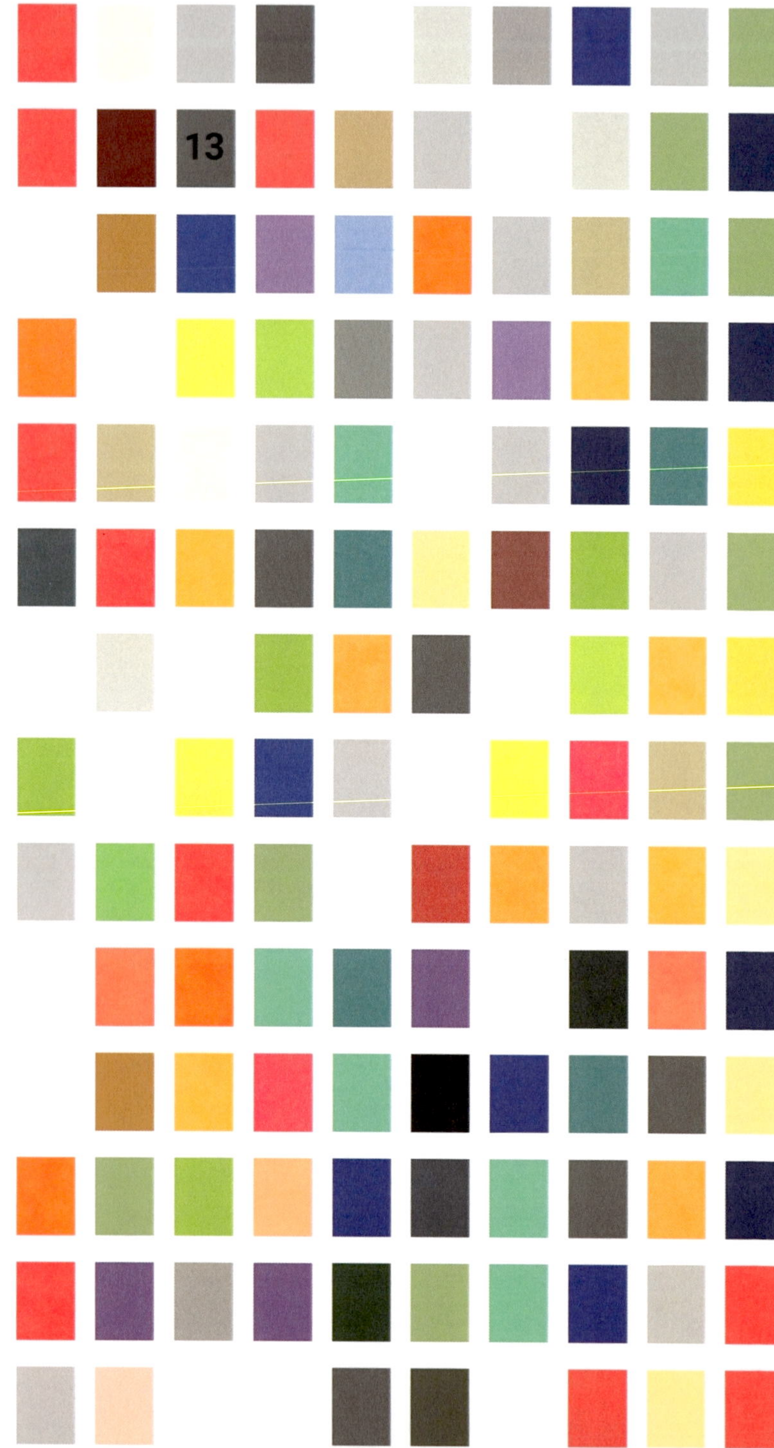

13

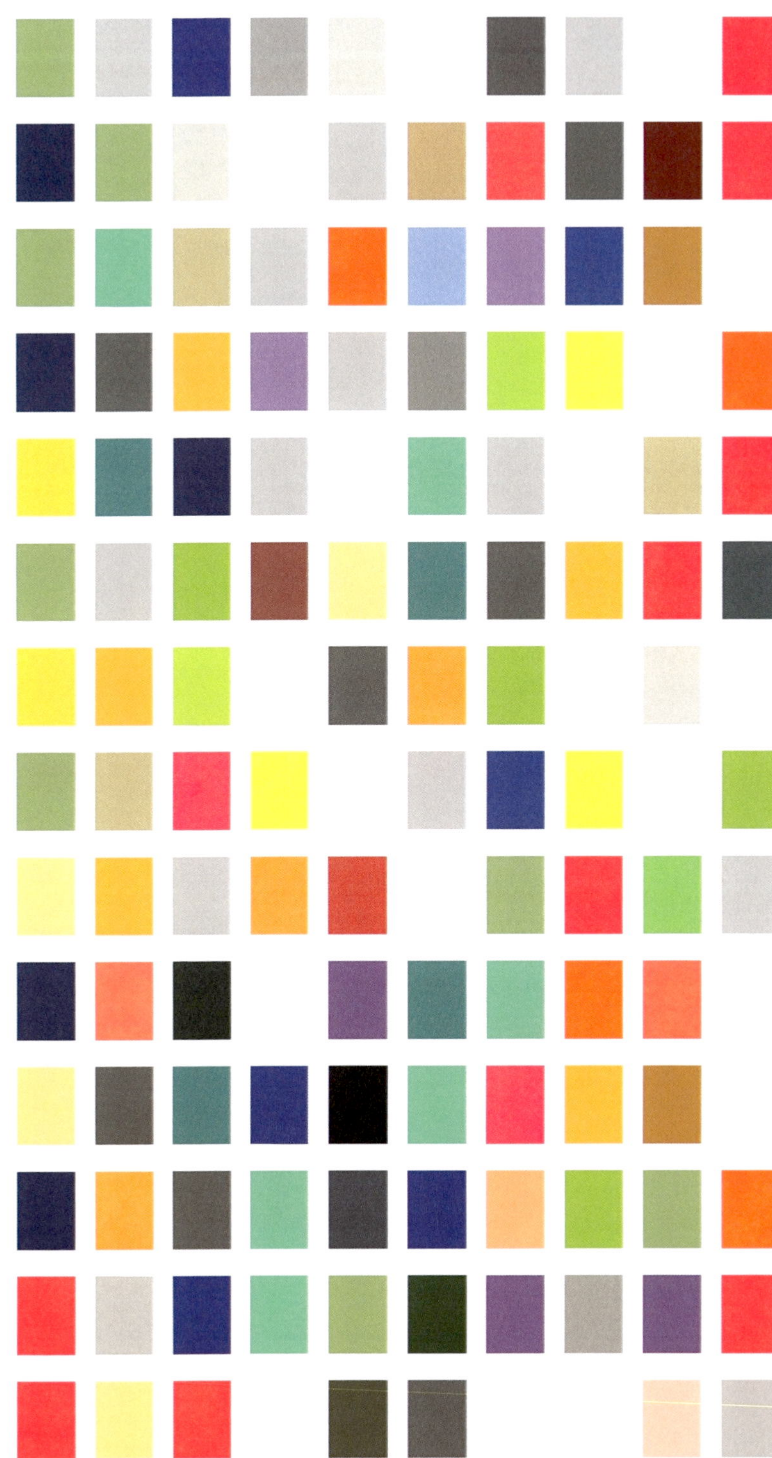

o that you were your selfe but love you are

no long er yours then you your selfe here live

a gainst this cum ming end you should pre pare

and your sweet sem blance to some o ther give

so should that beau ty which you hold in lease

find no de ter min a tion then you were

you selfe a gain af ter your selfes de cease

when your sweet is sue your sweet forme should beare

who lets so faire a house fall to de cay

which hus ban dry in hon our might up hold

a gainst the stor my gusts of win ters day

and bar ren rage of deaths e ter nall cold

o none but un thrifts deare my love you know

you had a fa ther let your son say so

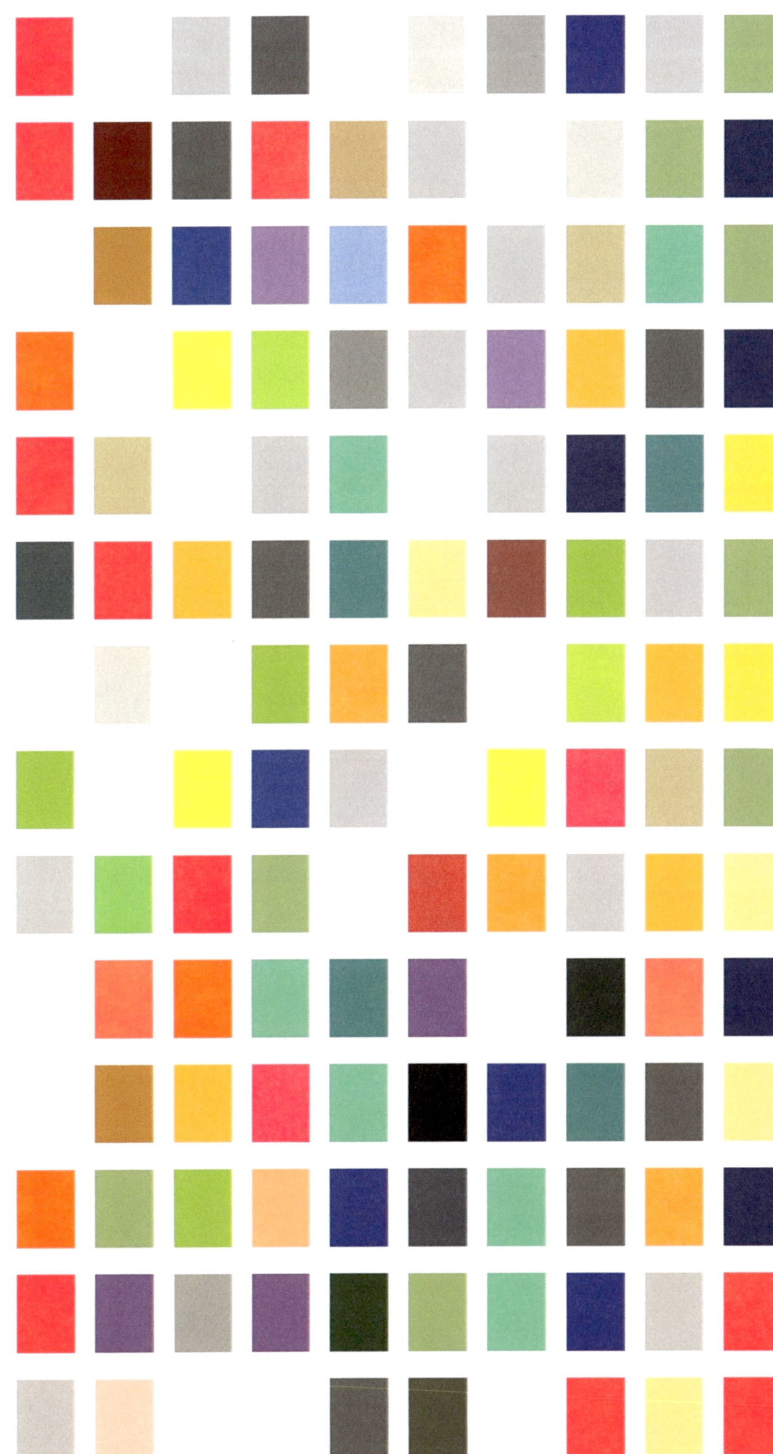

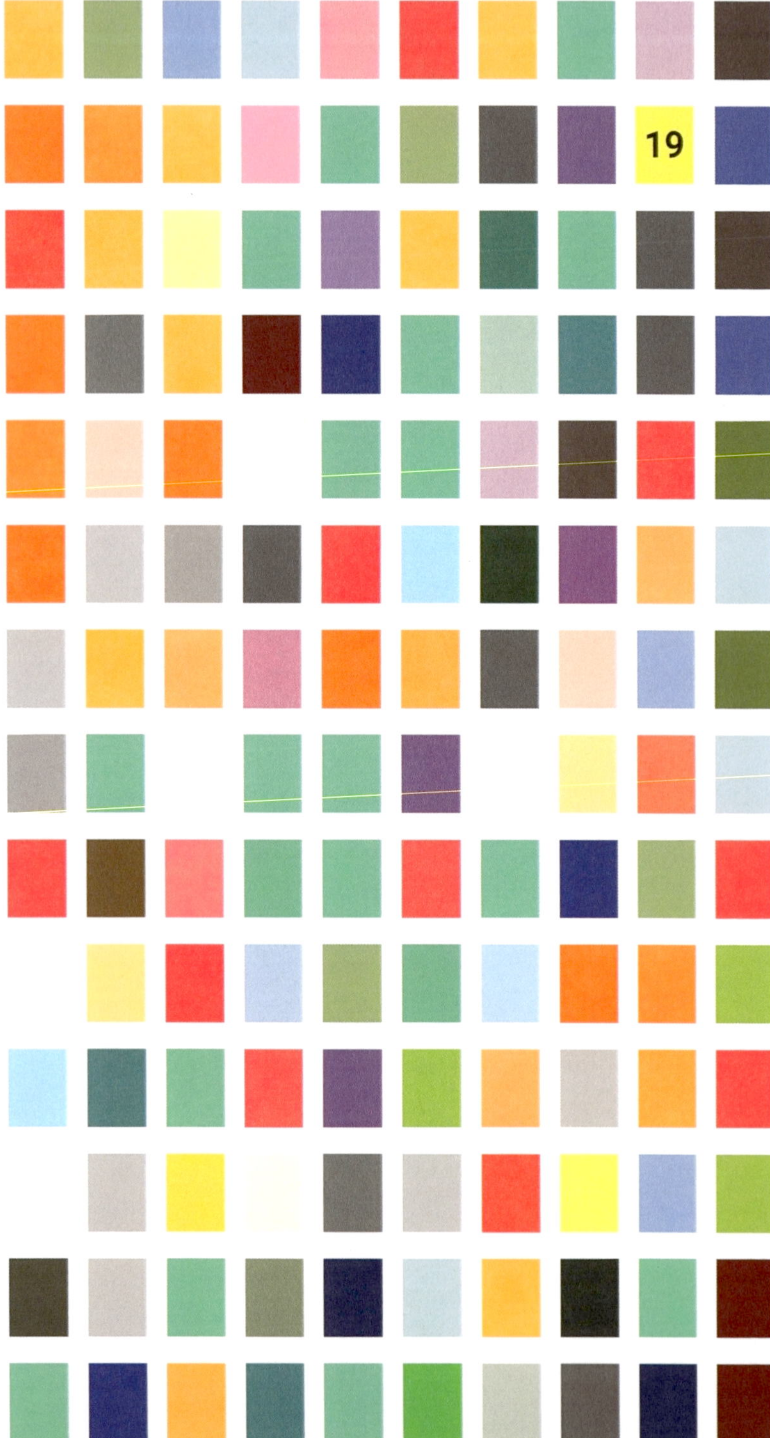

19

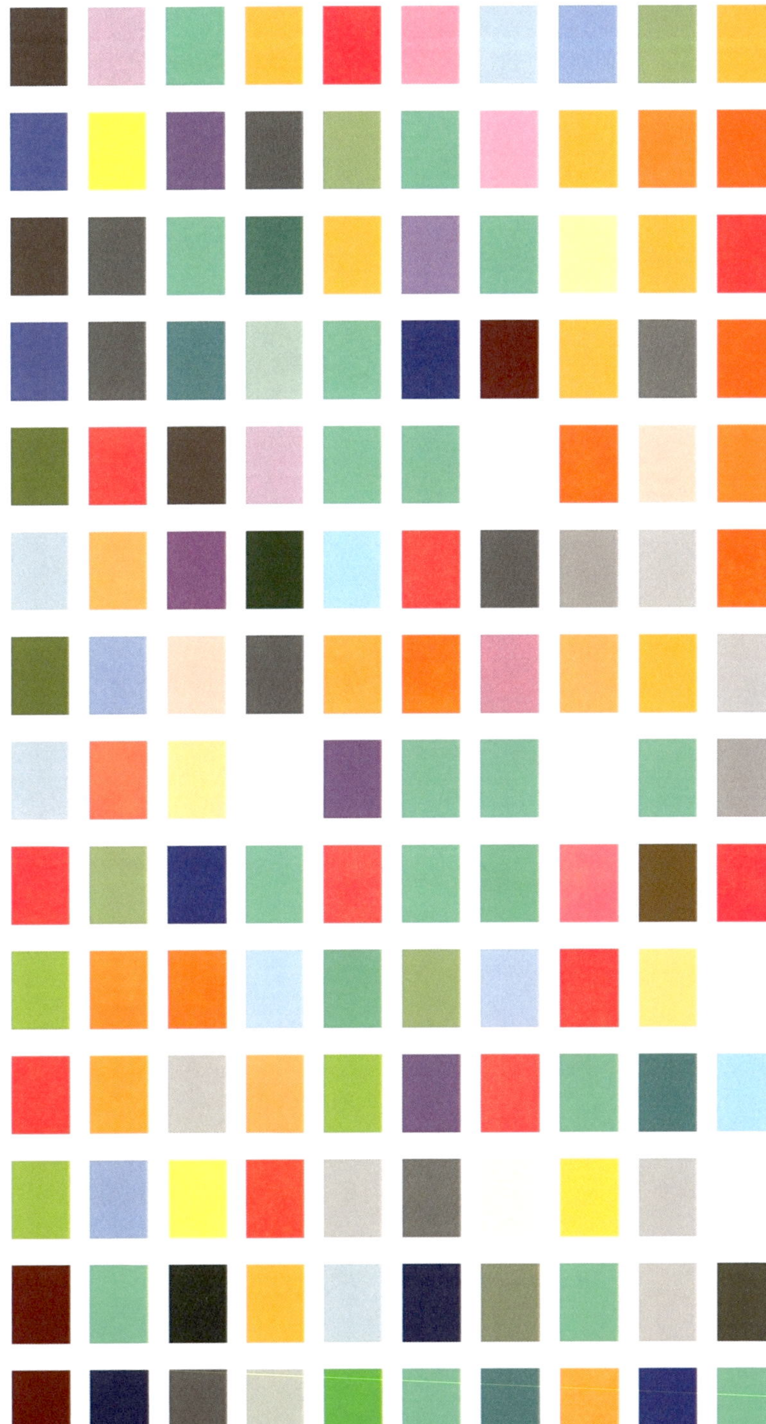

de vou ring time blunt thou the ly ons pawes

and make the earth de voure her owne sweet brood

plucke the keene teeth from the fierce ty gers jawes

and burne the long liv d phoe nix in her blood

make glad and sor ry sea sons as thou fleet st

and do what ere thou wilt swift foo ted time

to the wide world and all her fa ding sweets

but i for bid thee one most hei nous crime

o carve not with thy howers my love s faire brow

nor draw noe lines there with thine an tique pen

him in thy course un tain ted doe al low

for beau ties pat terne to suc cee ding men

yet does thy worst ould time dis pight thy wrong

my love shall in my verse e ver live young

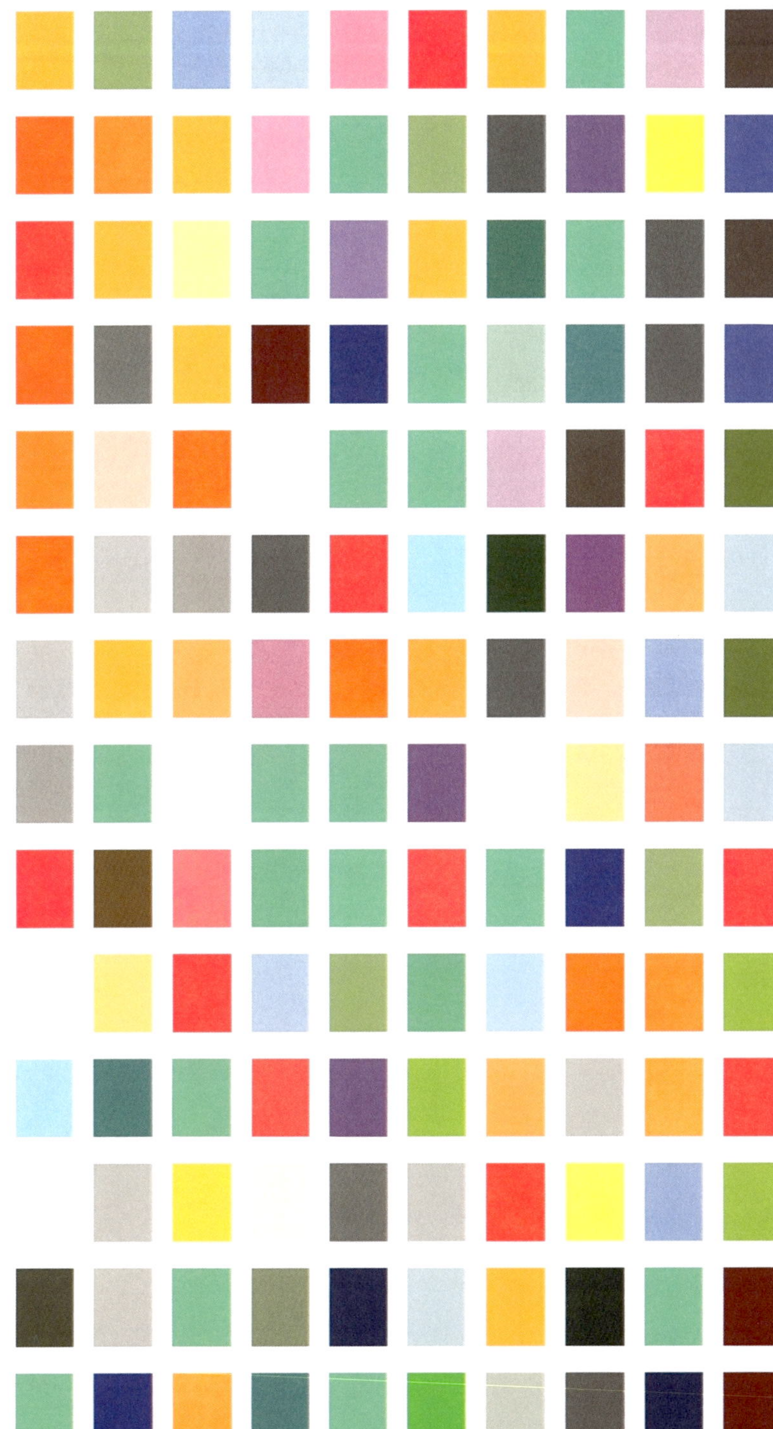

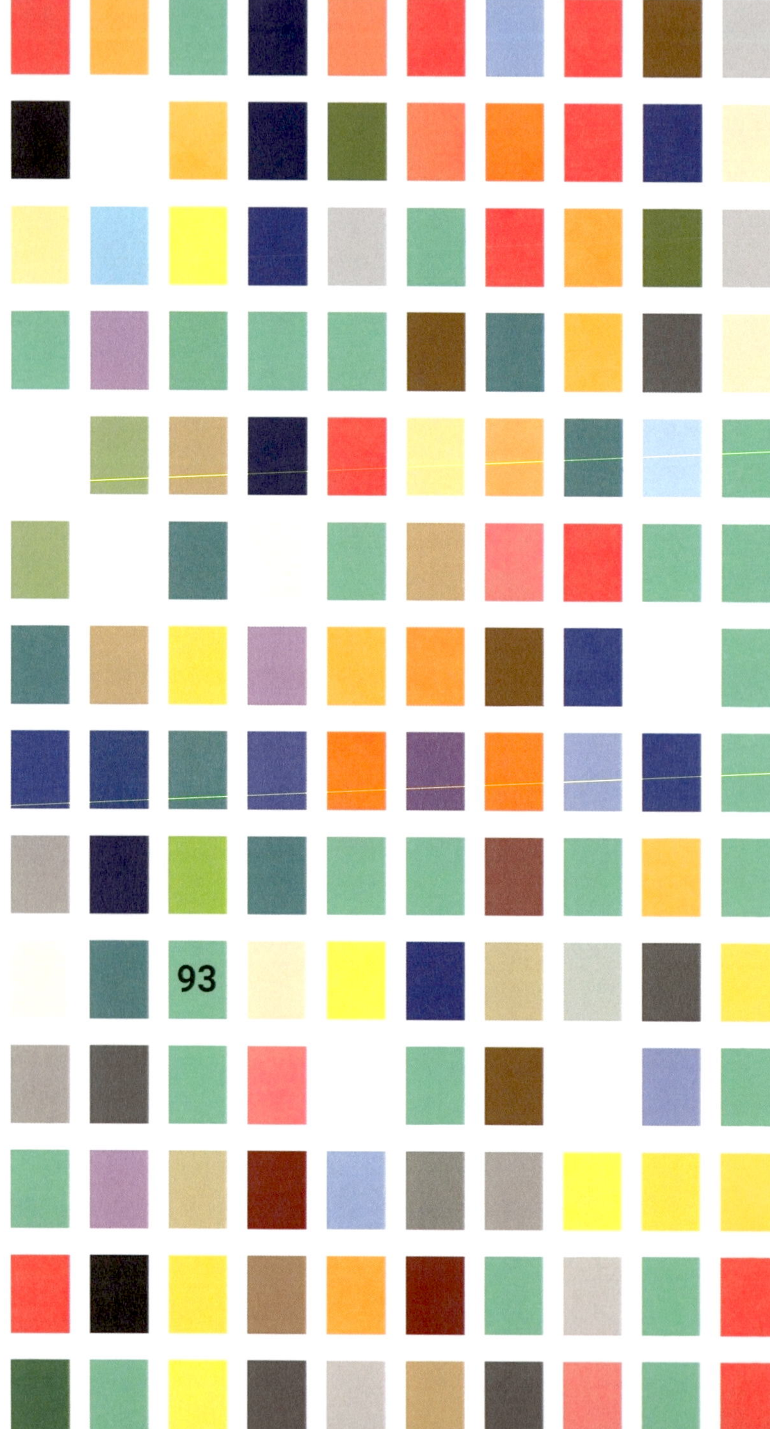

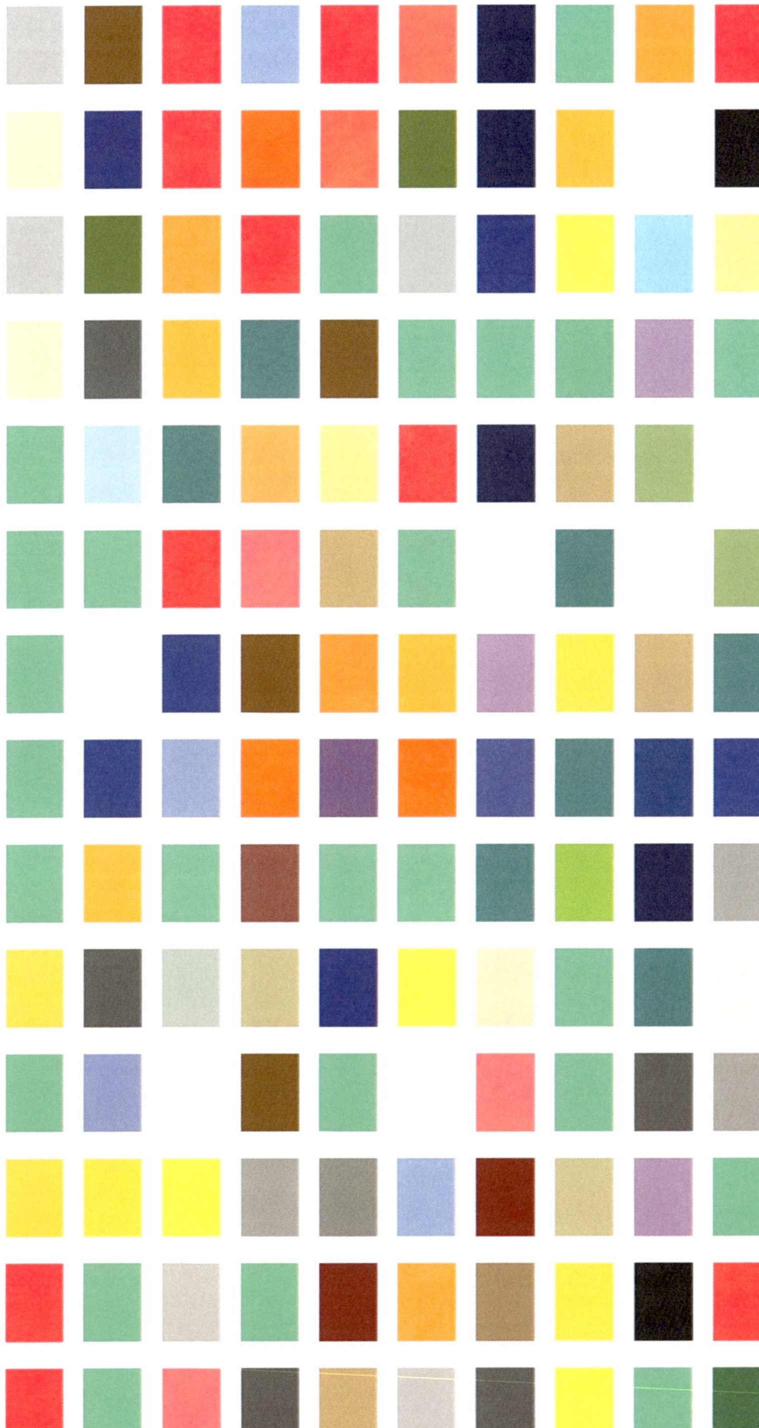

so shall i live sup po sing thou art true

like a de cei ved hus band so love s face

may still seeme love to me though al ter d new

thy lookes with me thy heart in o ther place

for there can live no ha tred in thine eye

there fore in that i can not know thy change

in man ies lookes the falce heart s his tor y

is writ in moods and frounes and wrinck les strange

but heaven in thy cre a tion did de cree

that in thy face sweet love should e ver dwell

what ere thy thoughts or thy heart s wor kings be

thy lookes should no thing thence but sweet nesse tell

how like eaves a pple doth thy beau ty grow

if thy sweet ver tue an swere not thy show

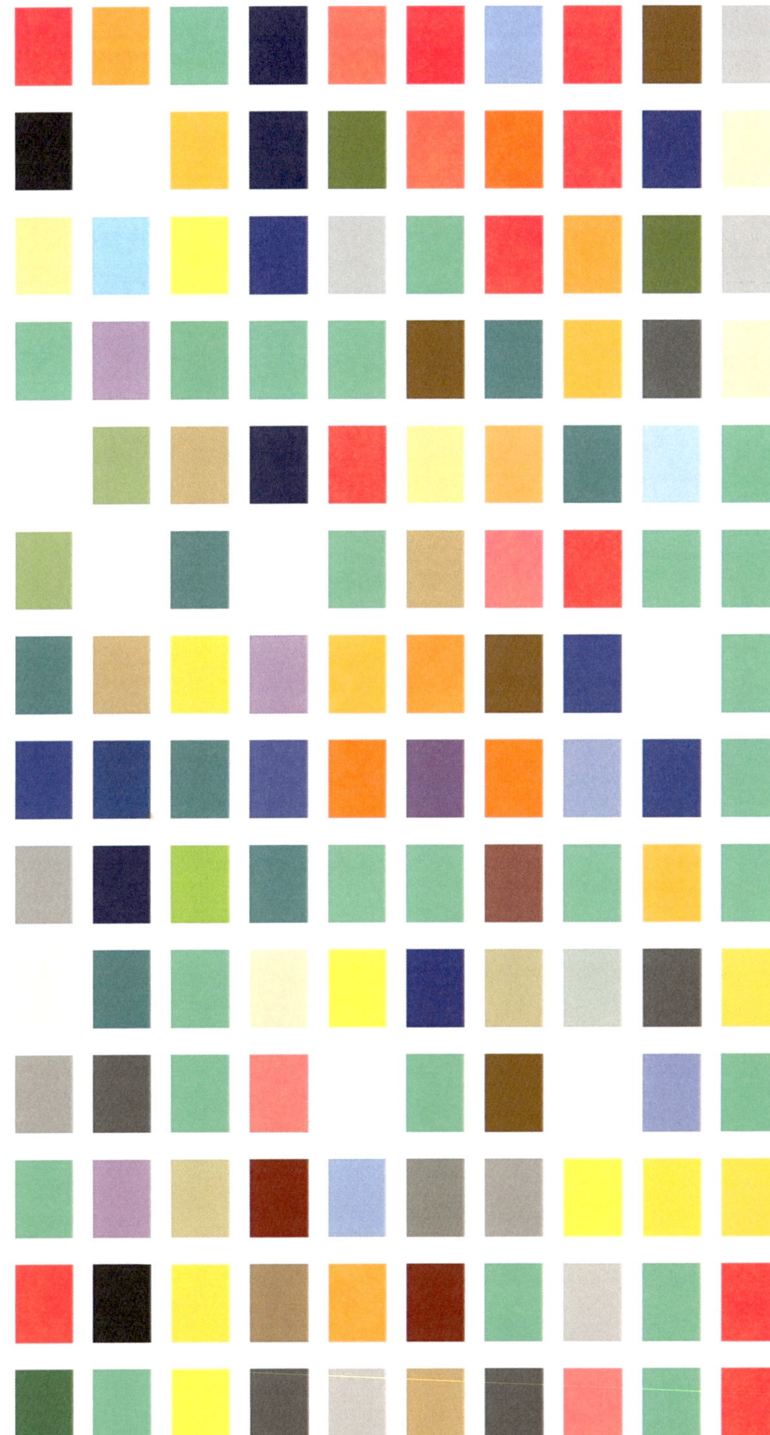

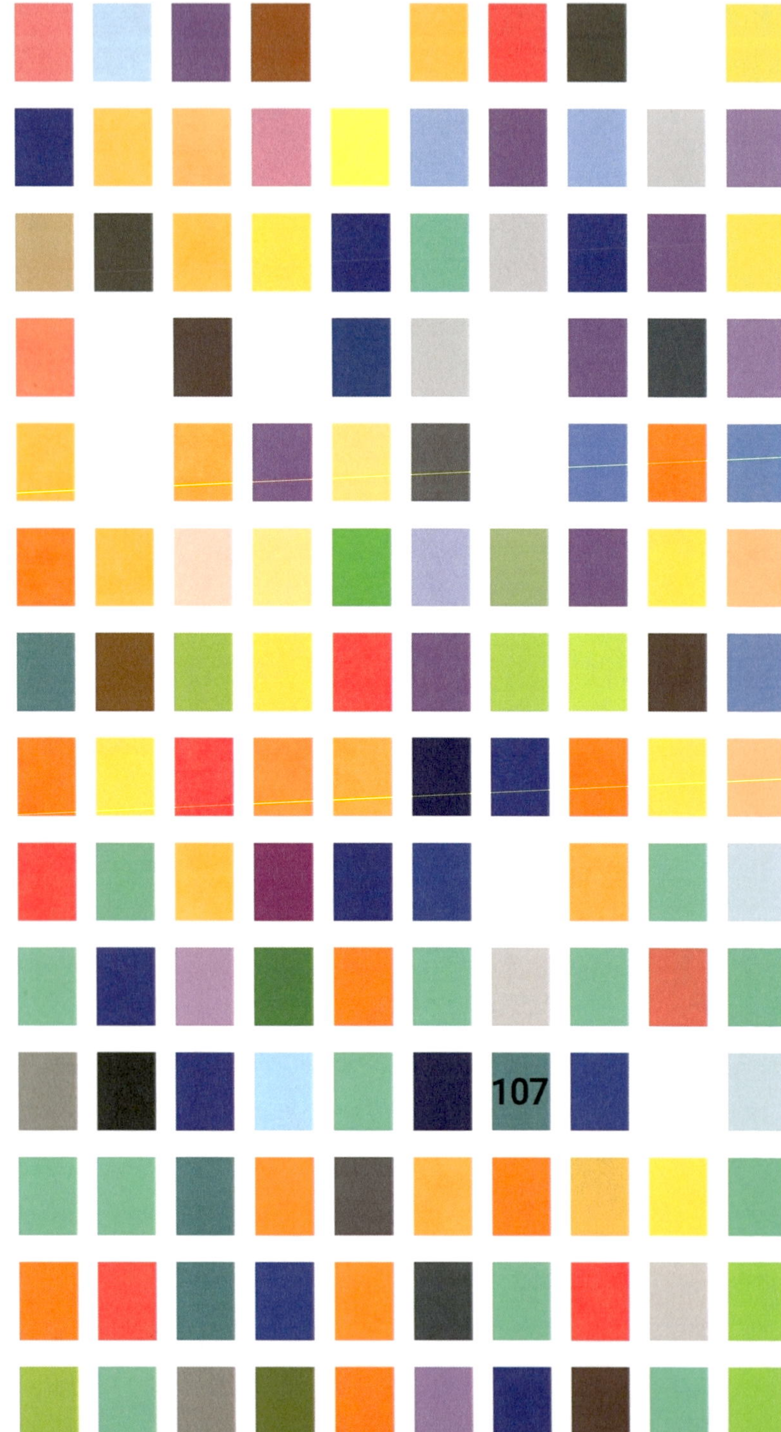

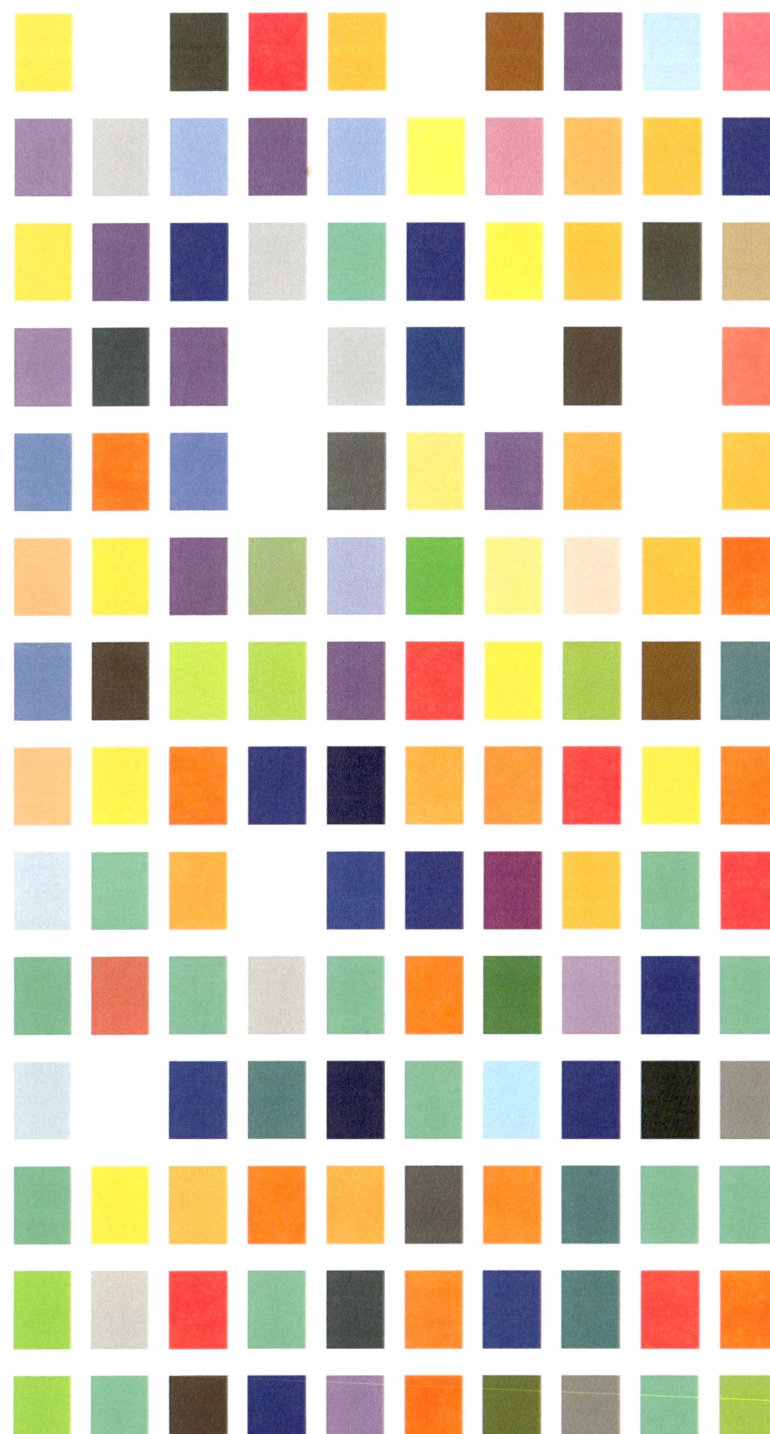

not mine owne feares nor the pro phe tick soule

of the wide world drea ming on things to come

can yet the lease of my true love con troule

sup posed as for feit to a con fin d doome

the mor tall moone hath her e clipse in dur de

and the sad au gurs mock their owne pre sage

in cer ten ties now crowne them selves as sur de

and peace pro claimes o lives of end lesse age

now with the drops of this most bal mie time

my love lookes fresh and death to me sub scribes

since spight of him ile live in this poore rime

while he in sults ore dull and speach lesse tribes

and thou in this shalt finde thy mon u ment

when tyr ants crests and tombs of brasse are spent

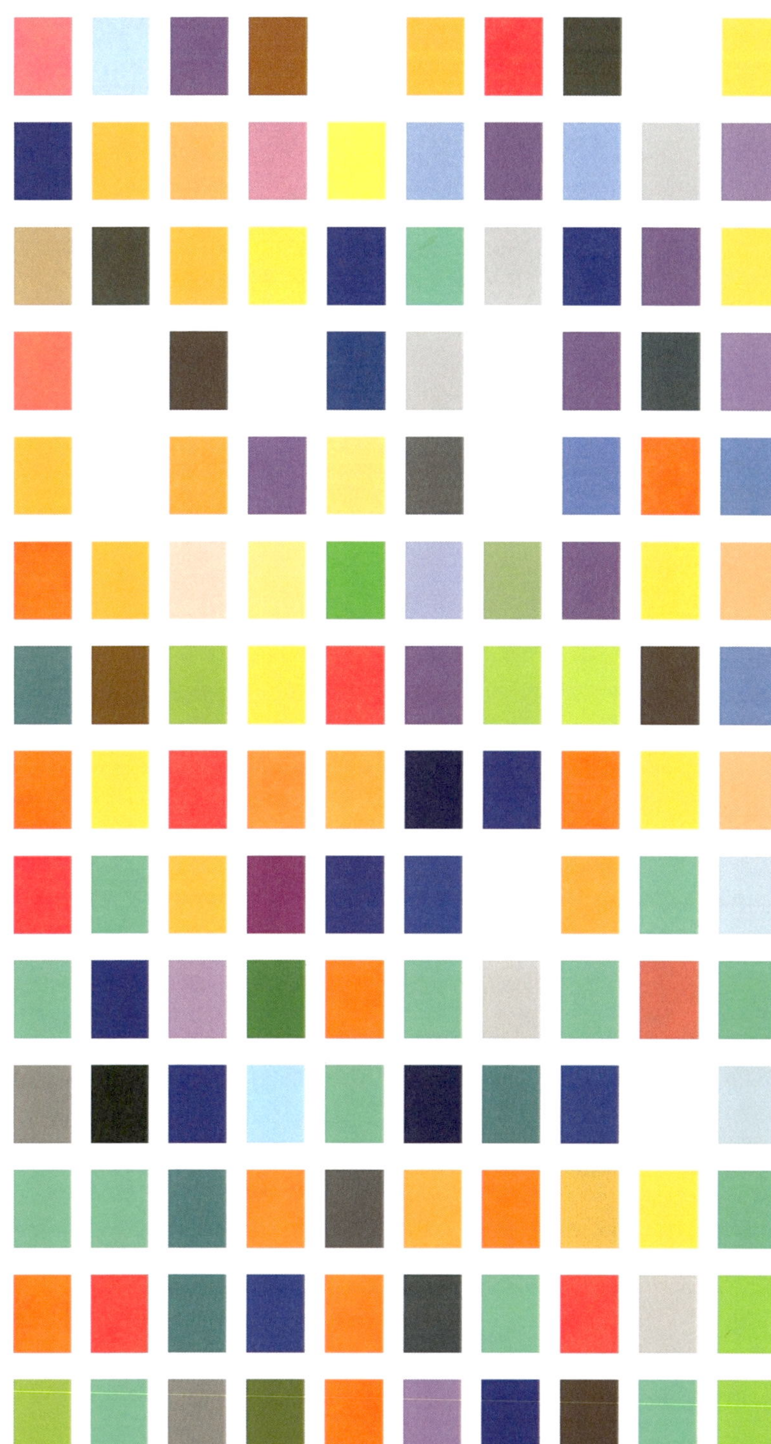

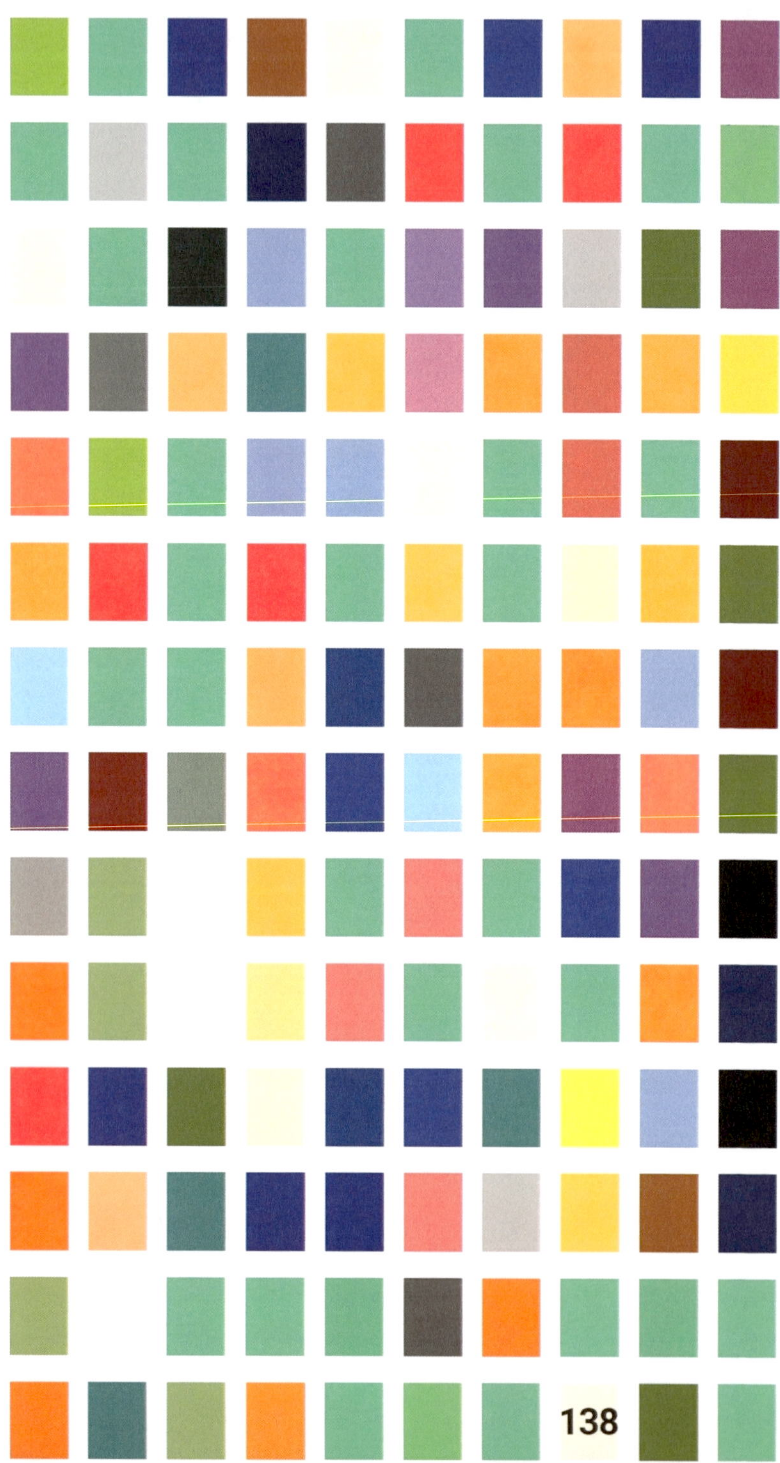

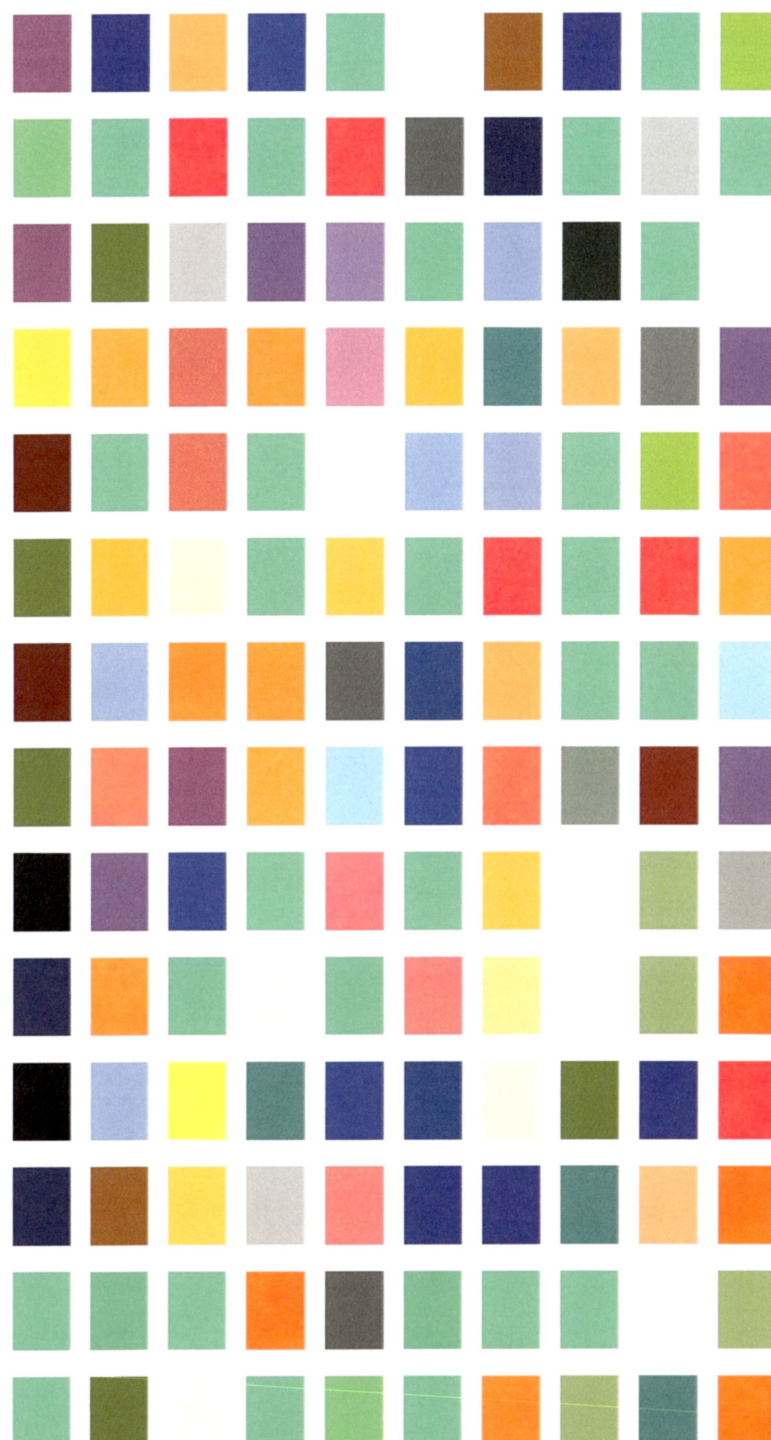

when my love sweares that she is made of truth

i do be leeve her though i know she lyes

that she might thinke me some un tut erd youth

un lear ned in the world s false sub til ties

thus vaine ly thin king that she thinkes me young

al though she knowes my dayes are past the best

sim ply i cre dit her false spea king tongue

on both sides thus is sim ple truth sup presst

but where fore says she not she is un just

and where fore sayes not i that i am old

o love s best ha bit is in see ming trust

and age in love loves not to have year es told

there fore i lye with her and she with me

and in our faults by lyes we flat tered be

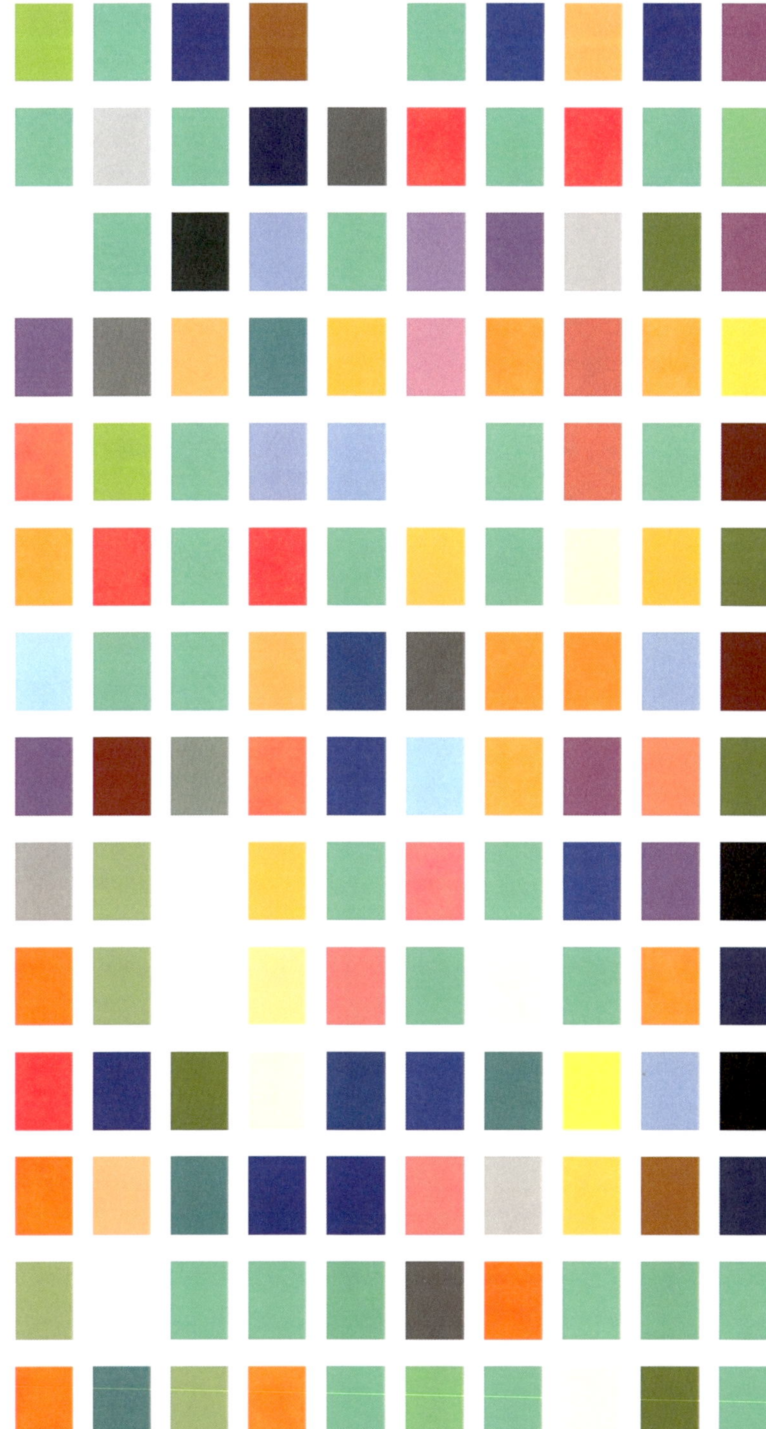

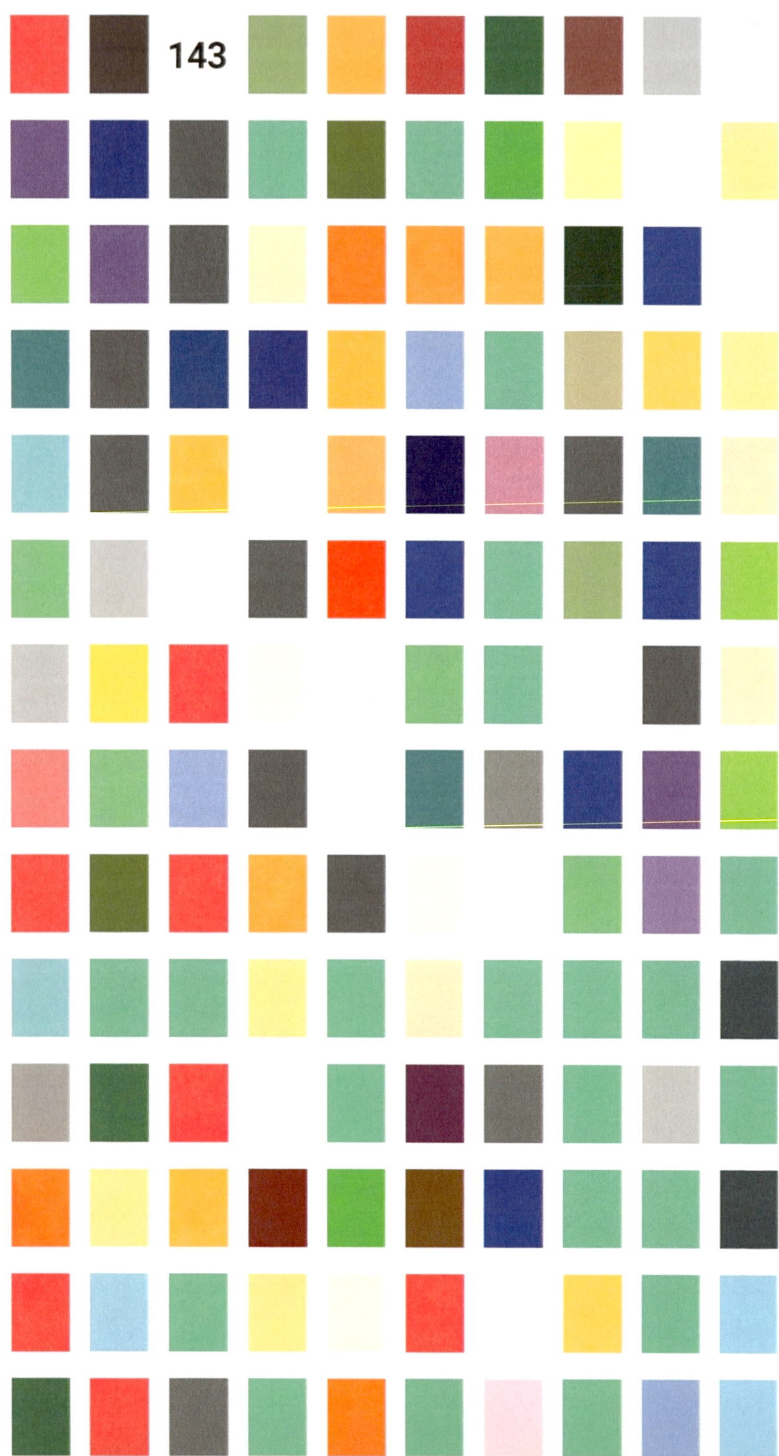
143

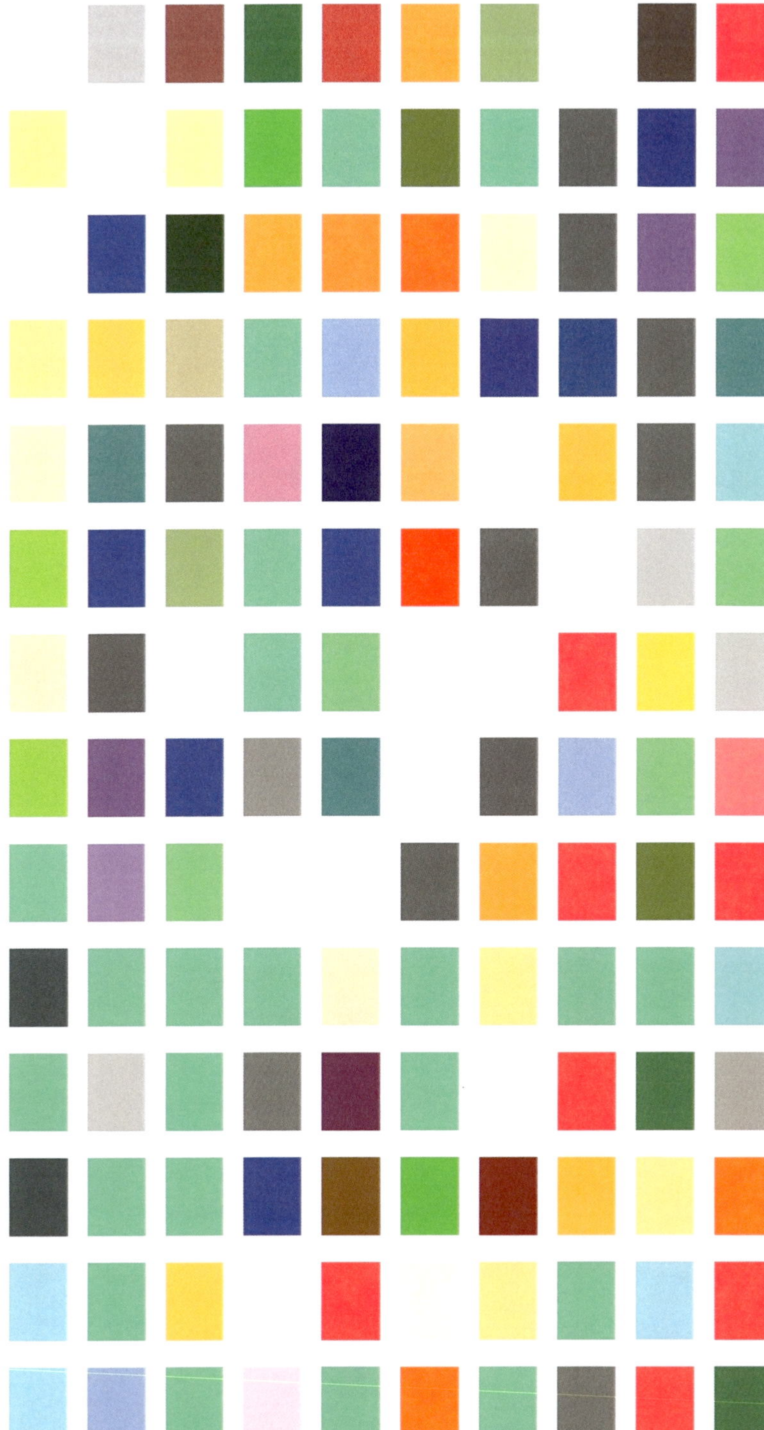

loe as a care full hus wife runnes to catch

one of her feth ered crea tures broake aw ay

sets downe her babe and makes all swift dis patch

in pur suit of the thing she would have stay

whilst her ne glec ted child holds her in chace

cries to catch her whose bus ie care is bent

to fol low that which flies be fore her face

not pri zing her poore in fant s dis con tent

so runst thou af ter that which flies from thee

whilst i thy babe chace thee a farre be hind

but if thou catch thy hope turne back to me

and play the mo ther s part kisse me be kind

so will i pray that thou maist have thy will

if thou turne back and my loude cry ing still

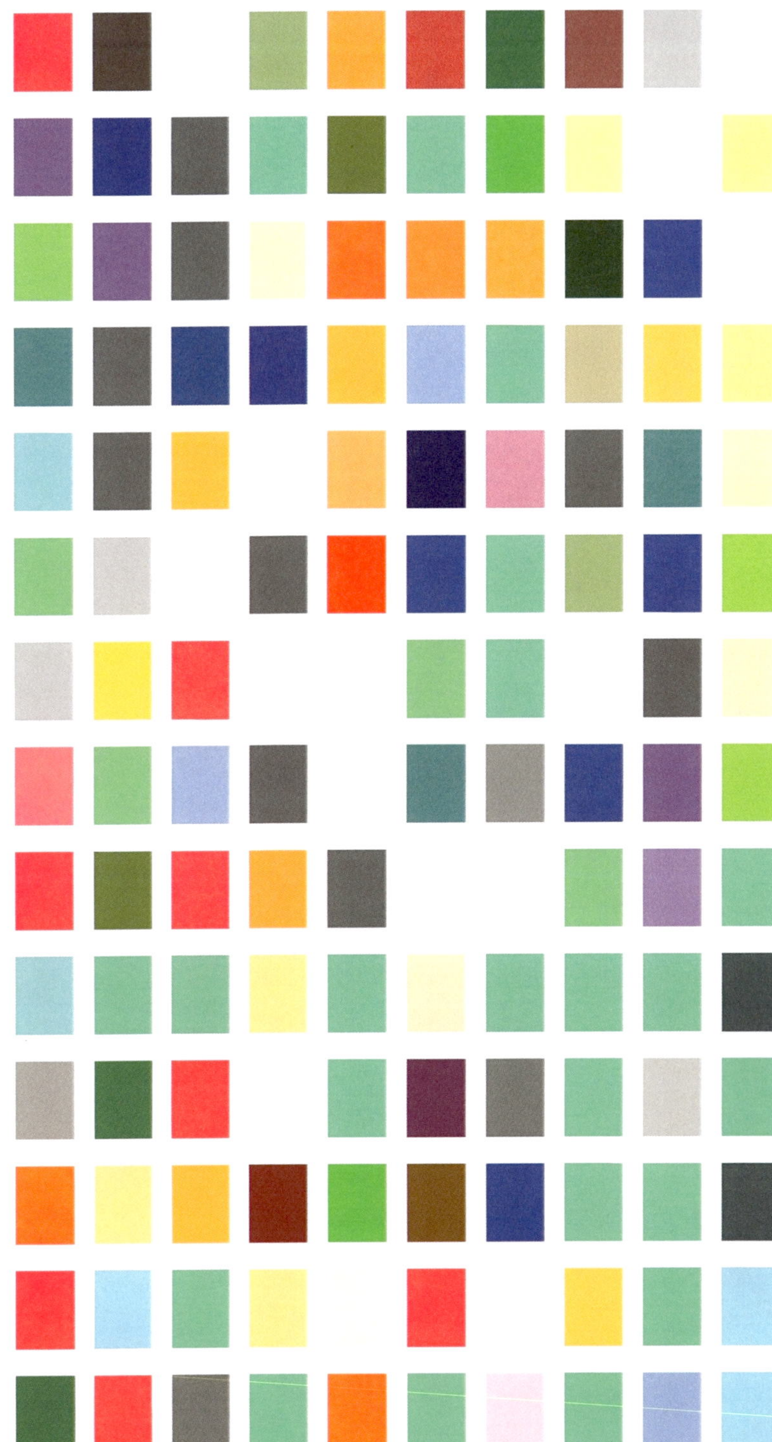

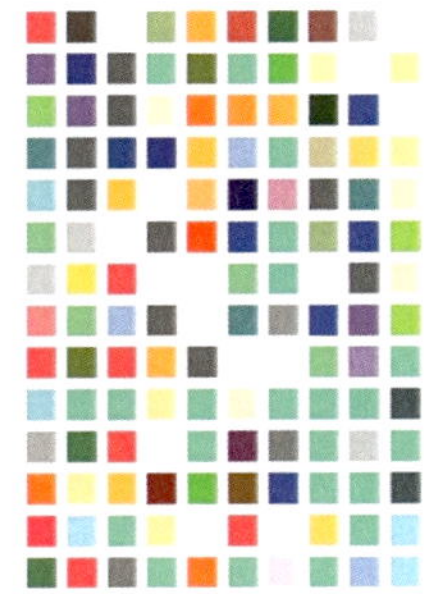

Notes:

Hold each page containing sonnet text up to light to reveal its BardCode surfacing from beneath.

The font used for the book's title is based on the handwriting of William Shakespeare. It is called William Shakespeare WF and is used with permission from Walden Font Co.

The colour used for the book's spine is Shakespeare / #5A96BB. Thanks to Franco Cortese for drawing our attention to this colour.

Pronunciation, where appropriate and unconventional to modern ears, arranged according to old pronunciations and scholarship ("heaven", for instance, as one syllable (i.e havn)— see Kerrigan, 1995).

All capitalisation and punctuation have been removed from the sonnets to emphasize their sound data.

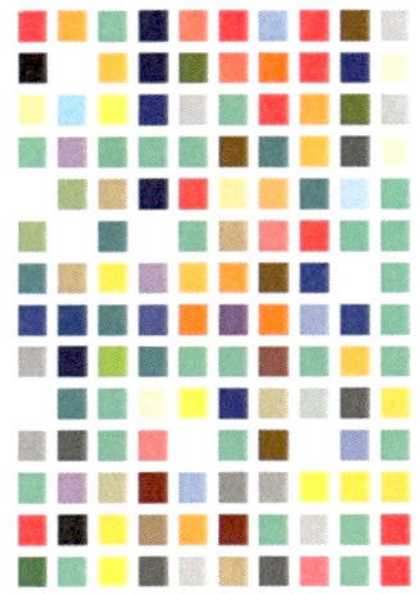

Gregory Betts is a poet, professor, editor, and musician. He is the author of seven previous books of poetry, two academic studies on the Canadian avant-garde, and editor of nine books of experimental writing.

This is his second response to the playground of Shakespeare's sonnets—the other being *The Others Raisd in Me*, in which he peels out 150 buried poems from the words and letters of Sonnet 150.

This book was fostered by Gary Barwin, Derek Beaulieu, Lisa Betts, Christian Bök, Natasha Pedros, Gyllian Raby, William Ralph (who provided key programming for the data visualizations), and Elizabeth Vlossak. Thanks to Gareth Jenkins for shaking this project from the trees, and spearing it to publication.

Betts teaches at Brock University in St. Catharines, Ontario, Canada.

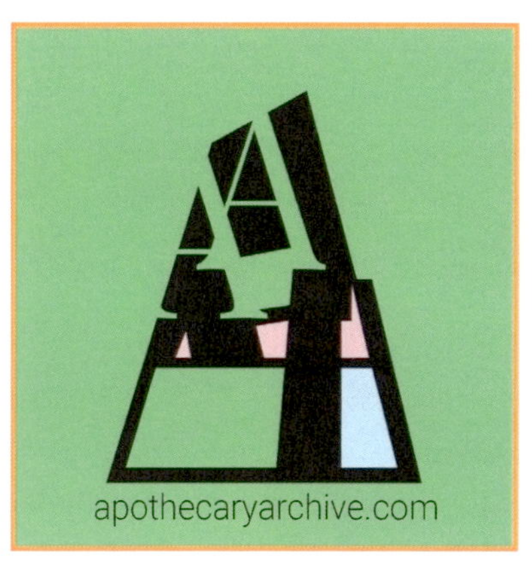

apothecaryarchive.com